Strategic Studies Institute
and
U.S. Army War College Press

RUSSIA'S CONTRIBUTION AS A PARTNER
IN THE WAR ON TERRORISM

Henry Plater-Zyberk

July 2014

*****

Comments pertaining to this report are invited and should be forwarded to: Director, Strategic Studies Institute and U.S. Army War College Press, U.S. Army War College, 47 Ashburn Drive, Carlisle, PA 17013-5010.

*****

This manuscript was funded by the U.S. Army War College External Research Associates Program. Information on this program is available on our website, *www.StrategicStudies Institute.army.mil*, at the Opportunities tab.

*****

The Strategic Studies Institute and U.S. Army War College Press publishes a monthly email newsletter to update the national security community on the research of our analysts, recent and forthcoming publications, and upcoming confer-ences sponsored by the Institute. Each newsletter also provides a strategic commentary by one of our research analysts. If you are interested in receiving this newsletter, please subscribe on the SSI website at *www.StrategicStudiesInstitute.army.mil/newsletter*.

FOREWORD

Russia's seizure of Crimea from Ukraine in March 2014 underscored the vast differences between the world views of Russia and the United States. Yet these differences notwithstanding, Russia and the United States do share key security challenges. One of these is terrorism. The 2014 Winter Olympics in Sochi, Russia, saw the attendance of a significant number of high-profile U.S. citizens at an event explicitly threatened by Islamic insurgents. This was seen to provide a prime opportunity for the two nations to foster meaningful cooperation against a common threat. Yet, the extent of joint work in counterterrorism with Russia remains insignificant.

Written before the Sochi Games, this monograph by Henry Plater-Zyberk explores the Russian approach to counterterrorism, and draws significant conclusions on the prospects for common cause with Russia in fighting terror. Cooperation with Russia in this field is possible and would provide significant benefits, but requires deep understanding of unique Russian concepts and constraints, and the specific nature of the terror threat perceived by Russia.

Mr. Plater-Zyberk provides these insights. This monograph is therefore recommended for policymakers considering all aspects of security cooperation with Russia.

DOUGLAS C. LOVELACE, JR.
Director
Strategic Studies Institute and
    U.S. Army War College Press

ABOUT THE AUTHOR

HENRY PLATER-ZYBERK retired from full-time research in 2011, and now serves as a Senior Research Fellow at the Prague Security Studies Institute. His previous assignment was with the United Kingdom (UK) Ministry of Defence's Conflict Studies Research Centre (CSRC) as a senior lecturer/analyst. During his career with CSRC, Mr. Plater-Zyberk wrote and briefed prolifically on political and internal security issues of Russia and other former Soviet states, regularly lecturing to the staff colleges and defense establishments of the UK and other North Atlantic Treaty Organization nations. Mr. Plater-Zyberk's service with the Royal Air Force Reserve was in a variety of roles that made use of his extensive language skills. Between assignments, he maintained his language skills and close contact with the targets of his research by assisting bilateral negotiations and direct military-to-military exchanges as a facilitator and multilingual interpreter. When writing on particularly sensitive topics, Mr. Plater-Zyberk also published under the pseudonym "Gordon Bennett." He is currently working on a comprehensive history of the Soviet and post-Soviet security and intelligence services. Mr. Plater-Zyberk graduated with a degree in Russian from the University of London.

SUMMARY

Key points resulting from this analysis include:

- Until the end of the Cold War, terrorism was a phenomenon practically unknown in the Soviet Union. The chaotic disappearance of the Union of Soviet Socialist Republics (USSR) resulted, among other developments, in two wars in North Caucasus and subsequent waves of terrorism in the region and terrorist attacks in Moscow. The demise of the USSR also weakened the organizations responsible for the security and law and order of Russia — a phenomenon rarely understood in the West.

- Russia and the United States are the priority targets for many radical Islamic groups. The two countries should be able, in theory at least, to cooperate closely against many terrorist groups. However, several issues, which each country sees as important, make this cooperation very difficult and occasionally impossible.

- In the post-communist, unipolar world, the United States was the dominant power, which paid little attention to the views and opinions of other countries. This attitude was particularly strongly resented in Russia, accustomed to its status of an equal security and military power. The United States failed to appreciate the changes in the Russian Federation and still does not always accept that repetitive public criticism of Russia's democratic deficit can be counterproductive.

- Political orphans of the Soviet Union, who regret the disappearance of the country they were born in, brought up in, and worked for, run

Russia. Twenty-three years after the collapse of communism, they may not want to see a return of communism, but they want the new Russia to be as respected or feared as was the USSR.

- Many Russians see the United States as the principal culprit of the USSR collapse and the present U.S. foreign policy as a continuing attempt to dominate the world. They also blame the United States and other Western countries for profiting from the chaos of their own making in the 1990s.

- The United States has a clear choice between imperfect cooperation with an imperfect Russia, or in-your-face lecturing of Moscow about its deficiencies. The lecturing achieved nothing positive so far and provoked Russian counterarguments about Washington's double standards.

- Anti-terrorist cooperation with Russia can be very productive if it is well planned and executed. This requires a detailed knowledge of those with whom to work, and with specific lists of operational do's and don'ts.

- For the last 12 years, the Russian security apparatus has benefitted from increased funding. While it has become more effective, this brings a duality, creating more problems not only for those against whom it operates, but also for potential partners. Russia has become, once again, a security superpower.

Successful anti-terrorist cooperation with Russia requires, above all, an understanding of Russia. (NOTE: This monograph was written before the 2014 Winter Games at Sochi, Russia.)

RUSSIA'S CONTRIBUTION AS A PARTNER IN THE WAR ON TERRORISM

INTRODUCTION

Terrorism is a blight that has affected Russia for almost 2 decades. Since the early-1990s, the North Caucasus has been ravaged by small-scale attacks such as pinpoint assassinations and kidnappings, up to large scale attacks on communities—most vividly illustrated by the attack on Beslan in 2004, which killed hundreds, the majority of whom were children. Attacks have emphasized both casualties and the disruption of authority by attacking not just prominent civic leaders, religious leaders, and military personnel in both blunt and sophisticated ways, but also the civilian population. Although the Chechen Republic was the center of this problem for many years, it has spread into neighboring regions and beyond. Outside of Chechen, terrorists have attacked Russian transport networks—including bombing aircraft and airports, such as the Domodedovo attack in 2011, and also attacking trains. Attacks have also been conducted in Moscow itself, again vividly illustrated by the attacks on the Nord-Ost theatre in 2002.

Although they are not the only source of terrorist activity in Russia, radical Islamic cells based in the Caucasus are seen by the Russian authorities to be the main source of such activity. Furthermore, Russian officials point to the succor given to these cells (in the form of financial support, equipment, and fighters) by international terrorist groups and networks. For Moscow, this poses a dual dilemma: It is both a domestic problem and yet simultaneously an international one.

Such characteristics will be familiar to U.S. and European authorities, who have also faced attacks by terrorists, and, on the face of it, suggest that the West and Russia have a common cause in fighting "international terrorism." Some senior Western officials have advanced the idea of developing practical cooperation in the fight against international terrorists. It is a feature, for instance, of the North Atlantic Treaty Organization (NATO)-Russia agenda—and one which has yielded some practical results. The Winter Olympics, held in the Caucasus in Sochi in 2014, offered an obvious point of focus for such cooperation.

Yet, if the agenda appears to coincide and offers a potential platform for developing a more practically cooperative relationship, the situation is complex. On the one hand, U.S.-Russian relations are riven with wide problems, practical and conceptual. The Russian leadership is critical of many U.S. foreign policy and military initiatives on the international stage, and skeptical about the sincerity of U.S. rhetoric about cooperation. Any cooperation against terrorism must also be seen in the light of a wider political and security context marred by recurring scandals most recently illustrated by Edward Snowden's asylum in Russia.

On the other hand, there are more specific questions relating directly to a counterterrorism agenda. This relates to the "domestic and yet international" duality of the question. As a result, there are important questions of mutual understanding and evaluation of counterterrorist operations. Coordination of definitions of the problem, as well as preferred solutions, may prove difficult.

This monograph explores these questions. First, it lays out detailed Russian definitions of terrorism, illustrating the important point that Russian understandings of this blight draw on a fundamentally different history from Western definitions. It then turns to look at the Russian security "pyramid," which sets out the relevant authority structure. The monograph first examines the roles of coordinating bodies such as the Security Council (SC) and the National Anti-Terrorist Committee (NAC), before looking in more depth at the individual organs involved in counterterrorism operations, particularly the Federal Security Service (FSB) and Ministry of the Internal Affairs (MVD). The monograph then explores the most important question for Russia in terms of terrorism: the North Caucasus, illustrating the extent of the problem, before sketching out the security situation regarding the Winter Olympic Games in Sochi. The monograph finally looks at the wider context of the relationship between Russia and the West, particularly the United States, and looks at the lengthy list of tensions. These problems have an important negative impact on the wider relationship between Russia and the West, one that reduces the possibility for real cooperation in counterterrorism.

DEFINING TERRORISM FROM THE COLD WAR TO TODAY

The Union of Soviet Socialist Republics (USSR) was largely terrorism free, in part because of the oppressive, but on the whole effective, security system and in part because the KGB (the State Security Committee) and its predecessors, which were the central organs for counterterrorism operations, defined terrorism as an anti-Western propaganda slogan, Thus:

> Terroristicheskiy akt—terrorist act. One of the most extreme forms of subversive activity carried out by

3

capitalist intelligence services, their agents and anti-Soviet elements within the country, consisting of the assassination of a state or public personality or representative of authority, or the infliction of grievous bodily harm on them, on the grounds of their state or public office, with the aim of disrupting or weakening Soviet authority.[1]

This official Soviet definition of a terrorist act was therefore a political and linguistic by-product of the Soviet struggle with armed independence movements after World War II. Once the armed groups fighting for the independence of their countries and/or against Soviet invaders were subdued, Moscow could not accept that any sane Soviet citizen would attempt to subvert their communist paradise without outside support.

The situation changed dramatically on January 8, 1977, when a group of Armenian radicals planted three bombs in Moscow, the first in a carriage of the Metro, the second in one of the capital's food shops, and the third near the main shopping complex in Moscow. The three attacks killed and wounded 37 people.[2] Soviet leaders were shocked. Yuri Andropov, the head of the KGB, described the attacks as the crime of the century.[3] The investigation of the attack was given absolute priority and no resources were spared — for a whole year, the KGB attached about 800 of its own students to assist the investigation because the original Soviet investigating team had only 30 people. The USSR was simply not prepared for these types of attacks.[4]

The roots of terrorism in modern Russia can be found in the later stages of the decline of the USSR and immediately after its demise. The collapse of the USSR resulted in a concatenation of circumstances that allowed terrorism to flourish not just across the Soviet republics but also within Russia itself.[5] The collapse of authority had a dual impact. As the power of the Communist Party of the Soviet Union slowly faded away and, with it, all the state organizations it controlled, especially the law enforcement and security organs, the economy became a free-for-all rather than a free market system. This weakening of state organizations and the emergence of the new, powerful, and rich individuals operating in untested economic waters resulted in a rapid growth of crime.[6]

At the same time, the Russian Soviet Federative Socialist Republic, by far the largest and the most dominant component of the USSR, was the only republic without its own security organization. Just before the collapse of the Soviet Union, Russia set up its own version of the KGB very late, on May 5, 1991.[7] The setting up of the new security organizations, especially in the various regions of Russia, was exceptionally difficult in the post-Soviet chaos. There was no legal framework to deal with "new" crimes and transgressions, which in the Soviet period were simply regarded as anti-Soviet activities and treated accordingly.

The strict control of firearms and other weapons of the Soviet era deteriorated rapidly. Weapons dumps were only inadequately guarded, or even not at all, and military units in some areas — especially in North Caucasus — were attacked and their weapons stolen. The armed forces and law enforcement organs were not able to control some parts of the Russian Federation because the decisionmaking system within the power structures practically collapsed, as did the military conscription system and the central funding system.

The legal vacuum left by the Soviet Union was matched by the situation in the security and law enforcement organizations. The sword and shield of the ruling Communist Party of the Soviet Union was gradually dismantled and weakened by the defection of its personnel to the private sector. The failed October 1993 coup against Boris Yeltsin made him weaken the whole security apparatus even further, transferring some personnel and functions to the inefficient and corrupt, but representing no threat to him, Ministry of Internal Affairs.[8]

Subsequent (endless) reforms of the security apparatus in post-Soviet Russia and the rolling reallocation of the anti-terrorist units and resources in the early- and mid-1990s, resulted in a further weakening of the situation. Many officers retired or were removed by local authorities hostile to Moscow.[9] As a result, the Russian Ministry of Defense and the Security Ministry, responsible for the police who briefly replaced the KGB and the Ministry of Internal Affairs, were desperately short-staffed and underequipped.[10] When President Yeltsin decided to transfer the elite unit "Vympel" — originally set up by the First Directorate (Intelligence) of the KGB — from the Presidential Security Service to the MVD, all members of the unit objected. On February 11, 1994, they met their new boss, Minister of Internal Affairs, Viktor Yerin. Although General Yerin offered to increase their salaries by 40 percent, none of the 500 experts accepted the offer — most of them resigned, 50 moved to the Main Protection Directorate or reapplied for the jobs in the Presidential Security Service, 30 moved to the Intelligence Service, and 30 moved to the Federal Counterintelligence Service.[11]

During this time, Islam filled this ideological and political vacuum in some parts of the former Soviet

Union. In the North Caucasus in 1999, there were about 110 registered Islamic educational establishments with teachers from Syria, Jordan, Egypt, and Saudi Arabia. Some of the Russian Islamic scholars were taught in the Middle East or North Africa.[12] By 1999, in Dagestan alone, there were 1,670 mosques, 25 madrassas, nine Islamic establishments of higher education, and 1,230 inhabitants of Dagestan studied in 10 Islamic countries.[13] The recruitment of Russian citizens by the Islamic organizations was well-organized and well-funded. In mid-1998, Saudi Arabia began to pay more attention regarding who its funds were going to in Russia. The most popular form of transferring money to Islamic groups in Russia were couriers who arrived carrying substantial sums of money legally and left the county without it.[14]

In this post-Soviet chaos, legislative changes were made to the definition of terrorism. A new article (213.3) was introduced to the old Penal Code of the Russian Soviet Federative Socialist Republic. The new article described terrorism as:

> an explosion, arson, or other activities aiming to violate public security or to influence decisions of the authorities creating a danger of the loss of life, significant property damage, as well as other serious consequences.[15]

The new article envisaged — in the most extreme cases — the death penalty and the confiscation of property. Article 205 of the new Criminal Code introduced in 1996 and updated several times describes a terrorist act as:

> 1. An explosion, arson or other acts, frightening people and endangering the lives of people, causing significant property damage or other serious consequences,

in order to influence decision-making authorities or international organizations, as well as the threat to commit such acts for the same purposes — punishable by imprisonment for a term of 8 to 12 years. (Part One, as amended by the Federal Law of 27.07.2006 N 153-FZ.)

2. The same acts: a) committed by a group of persons, by prior collusion or by an organized group; b) resulting, inadvertently, in death of a person, and c) resulting in significant property damage or other grave consequences, shall be imprisoned for a term of 10 to 20 years. (Part Two, as amended by the Federal law from 30.12.2008 N 321-FZ.)

3. Acts stipulated in the first or second paragraph of this Article, if they: a) involve an attack on nuclear facilities or using nuclear materials, radioactive substances, sources of radiation or toxic, poisonous, hazardous chemical or biological agents, and b) caused intentionally death of a man — shall be imprisoned for a term of 15 to 20 years or life imprisonment. (Federal law of 30.12.2008 N 321-FZ.)[16]

Later, Vladimir Putin further amended the legislation, the Federal Law N 35-ФЗ (Nr 35-F3), "On Countering Terrorism," signed by President Putin on March 6, 2006, after it was ratified by both chambers of the Russian Parliament. Point 1 of Article 3 Describes terrorism as an ideology of violence and the practice of influencing decisions of public authorities, local governments or international organizations by terrorizing the population, and/or other forms of unlawful acts of violence.[17] The law specifies, among other things, what constitutes a terrorist act (Article 3); outlines the basis of the combat against terrorism (Article 5); describes the rules governing the use of the Armed Forces of the Russian Federation in the fight against terrorism permitting them to operate outside the

Russian territory (Articles 6 and 10); and gives them the power to shoot down aircrafts, in extreme situations (Article 7); the role and functions of those leading an anti-terrorist operation (Article 13); the competences and powers of the operational headquarters (HQs); and lawful infliction of harm in anti-terrorist operations (Article 22).[18]

THE RUSSIAN SECURITY PYRAMID

The Russian president, in accordance with Article 5 of Nr 35-F3, defines the main directions of the counterterrorist state policy and determines the composition of the operational HQ in anti-terrorist operations (Article 14).[19] He is the pinnacle of the law enforcement pyramid, dominating all the relevant core structures. These include the Security Council of the Russian Federation (SC) and the National Anti-Terrorist Committee (NAC).

The president forms and leads the SC. In the early- and mid-1990s, anti-terrorist operations were coordinated by the SC. President Boris Yeltsin established the Council in the summer of 1992. The main tasks of the Council were and remain:

- Preparation of the annual report of the President to the SC about Russia's security, as the key policy document for the organs of the executive power concerning the internal, external, and military policies, as well as drafting legal acts to protect vital interest of individuals, society, and the state from external and internal threats.
- Organizing the work of temporary and permanent interdepartmental commissions formed by the SC, on a functional and regional basis,

as the main instrument of developing the draft decisions of the President of the Russian Federation.

- Developing proposals to protect the constitutional sovereignty and territorial integrity of Russia. The SC also implements presidential strategic security programs.

The attack on the school in Beslan, Russia, in early-September 2004, provoked a deep reassessment of the Russian security strategy and showed the need for a new organization focusing only on the suppression of terrorism. In the wake of this, the role of the SC has grown considerably: The latest status, approved by the Russian President — the Chairman of the Council — on May 6, 2011, and updated on July 8, 2013, describes precisely the roles of President (Chairman) and the Secretary of the Council and gives both specific and wide powers.[20] The SC's responsibilities now cover all aspects of national security.

The SC brings together the heads of the main organs responsible for combating terrorism. These are the Federal Security Service the Ministry of Internal Affairs (MVD), the Foreign Intelligence Service (SVR), the Federal Protection Service (Federalnaya Sluzhba Okhrany or FSO), and the Ministry of Defence (MO).[21] Article 6 of the Law "On Countering Terrorism" of March 6, 2006, describes the role of the armed forces in combating terrorism, but the SC and the five organizations mentioned earlier represent the backbone of the Russian anti-terrorist machinery.

The National Anti-Terrorist Committee.

As President, Putin has restored the pre-eminence of the FSB and gradually reformed the whole security and law enforcement system. The Presidential Decree of February 15, 2006, Nr 116, set up the National Antiterrorist Committee (NAC), with the head of the FSB as its statutory chairman. In accordance with the decree, the NAC has its own operational HQ and operational HQs are also established in the regions. The leadership of the Federal HQ is nominated by the Chairman of the NAC, i.e., the President of Russia, and the heads of the local HQs are the regional heads of the FSB, unless decided otherwise by the President. The decree specifically mentions Chechnya (Point 4.1.) as an area of particular attention.

The decisions made by the Federal HQ have to be obeyed on Russian territory, and the relevant decisions of the local HQs, in accordance with their competence, have to be obeyed by all regional state organs. The person in command of the joint group of forces at the federal level is the Minister of Internal Affairs. The decree addresses also the process of the withdrawal of troops from Chechnya. The apparatus of the NAC is in the FSB system (Point 11a). The staff size of the FSB is to be increased by 300 places and that of the FSO by seven places. (Point 13). The regional HQs were to be organized very quickly.[22]

The decree was updated on August 3, 2006, and November 4, 2007, giving the NAC the power to cooperate with other countries in combatting terrorism, and involving it in planning of the protective measures for people fighting terrorism and victims of terrorism. Further updates, concerning the personnel of the Federal HQ and the regional HQs, appeared on August 8, 2008, April 22, 2010, and October 8, 2010.[23]

The main body coordinating the everyday operations and other organs is the FSB, a much depleted successor of the Soviet KGB.[24] This role was originally based on the law "On Combating Terrorism" of July 25, 1998, Nr 130-F3, amended several times and later replaced by the law "On Countering Terrorism" of March 10, 2006, Nr 35-F3.[25] Much maligned by its enemies and opponents in Russia and abroad, the FSB, helped by Putin's patronage, is the best trained, best equipped, and the most efficient security organ in Russia.

The FSB also plays a major role countering terrorism in the regions. The FSB's anti-terrorist Special Purpose Centre was established on October 8, 1998, and includes Russia's two best anti-terrorist units known today as Directorate "A" (Alfa group) and Directorate "V" (*Vympel* group). On July 16, 1999, the center acquired the Special Operation Service (changed later to "Directorate"). The center serves as Russia's main anti-terrorist establishment and the FSB operational unit.[26]

The heads of the FSB's operational HQs, in accordance with the Presidential Decree Nr 116 of February 15, 2006 (as amended), are the heads of the regional FSB directorates, with the exception of Chechnya, where the priority has been given to the Ministry of Internal Affairs where its police force and the Internal Troops provide the frequently used firepower.[27]

The Law Nr 40-F3 of April 3, 1995, allows the FSB to have official contacts with foreign special services — implying both intelligence and security organizations — and law enforcement agencies. The law gave the FSB the right to cooperate with foreign partners within the framework of the established rules and international agreements. The service has 142 such contacts from 86 countries and has its own official representatives in 45 countries.[28]

Powerful politically, reasonably well equipped, better trained and disciplined than other organizations combating terrorism in Russia, the FSB nevertheless is an awkward partner for all foreign potential security organizations, especially those in NATO countries. All eight directors and one minister responsible for the FSB and its two predecessors, in the short history of the Russian Federation, were educated in the Soviet educational system belonging to one of its power structures. The last four heads of the FSB started their careers in the KGB, as did all six commandants of the highly regarded FSB academy. They may not see the United States as the enemy, but the new generations of the security personnel formed by them trusts the United States no more than did their predecessors. Equally, cooperation with the FSB is also difficult because it operates against real and imaginary spies and enemies of the state in Russia and does it usually effectively but without much finesse. It is therefore very often criticized by the Western media and human rights organizations.

The Ministry of Internal Affairs.

The Russian MVD is seen by some countries as the alternative Russian partner when it comes to fighting terrorism. The May 2013 visit to the United States of the Russian Minister of Internal Affairs was a moderate success. During the meeting with the head of the Homeland Security Department, Janet Napolitano, Minister General Vladimir Kolokoltsev called for the creation of a joint U.S.-Russian working group to counter crime and terrorist threats, and praised the existing, but insufficient according to him, cooperation. "Since the beginning of this year, we have exchanged 827 documents with U.S. law enforcement agencies," Kolokoltsev told reporters, adding that the United States is one of the top five countries with which Russia cooperates within Interpol.[29]

Additionally, the MVD wants to improve cooperation with the United States in tackling cyber crime, especially searching for the Internet Protocol (IP) addresses of attackers threatening the cyber security of the two countries.[30] This may be the only—and limited—opportunity for both sides, as the FSO, the Russian principal cyber and electronic security operator, and the FSB would be unlikely to join. The agreement on cooperation in cyberspace was close to final approval at the beginning of this year. The United States and Russia were to cooperate in combating attacks on computer networks of state agencies. In case of detection of any activity that can potentially damage the national security, Russian and American specialists would be able to contact each other using a special communication line to deal with the threat together.[31]

Cooperation with the MVD is politically and operationally less risky than working with the FSB, but there are serious drawbacks. First, the MVD has been very corrupt in its Soviet period and the post-Soviet era. During the failed October 1993 coup, the MVD supported Boris Yeltsin, saving his career and possibly his life. It was rewarded with full presidential support and better funding—but not with the quality control which it badly needed. Russia was economically weak and flooded by a crime wave. The sweeping reforms of the ministry's 1.2 million-strong police force, notorious for its corruption, came only in 2011. Some 200,000 officers were dismissed, salaries were raised and the force changed its name from "militia" to "police."[32]

Second, the MVD's capacities are limited. The MVD's own anti-terrorist structure, the Main Directorate for Combating Extremism of the MVD, was established by Presidential Decree Nr 1316 on September 6, 2008, and was updated twice in 2011. The Directorate is the main operational unit of the ministry responsible for combating extremism and terrorism. It takes part in formulating policies countering extremism and terrorism, and organizes and coordinates within it competent MVD structures and executive powers in the regions.[33] The MVD is also in charge of the Internal Troops and their seven regional commands.[34] They are a relic of the old Soviet era, and their robust presence, sadly necessary, is a testimonial of Russia's terrorist and criminal problems. Internal Troops sustained heavy losses in North Caucasus since the beginning of the first Chechen war and will continue to be deployed in the region irrespective of the level of tension there. The Internal Troops are responsible for:

- Maintaining public order, together with the MVD police.
- Combatting terrorism and handling the legal aspects of the anti-terrorist activities.
- Protection of important public facilities and special cargo.
- Taking part in the territorial defense of the country.
- Assisting the FSB border guards.[35]

The ministry's information acquisition capabilities are limited, and its listening and electronic surveillance capacities are modest, in comparison with the FSO, the MO, or the FSB. It has limited experience dealing with foreign security related issues and its counterintelligence activities, including monitoring foreign contacts, are handled by the FSB. Cooperation with the MVD is the safest but also the second best choice. All this machinery is enforcing law and security on the territory of the Russian Federation, but its main effort is focused on terrorist centers in the North Caucasus and Volga regions.

If an awareness of these different elements of the Russian security pyramid is important, at the same time, we cannot escape the central role of the president. Putin is uncompromising. In September 1999, as newly appointed Prime Minister, Putin said publically that terrorists will be pursued and killed, even if they are in the toilet.[36] On November 12, 2002, following a summit meeting between Russia and the European Union (EU), when challenged by a journalist about the war in Chechnya, Putin said:

> If you want to become a complete Islamic radical and are ready to undergo circumcision, then I invite you to Moscow. We are a multi-denominational country. We have specialists in this question as well. I will recommend that he carry out the operation in such a way that after it nothing else will grow.[37]

In July 2003, after a suicide bombing at a rock festival, Putin said: "They must be dug up out of their basements and caves, where they are still hiding, and destroyed."[38] At the end of March 2010, after the terrorist attacks in the Moscow metro, he declared:

> . . . in this case, we know that they [terrorists] are lying low. This is a matter of honor of the law enforcement organs — to dig them out from the bottom of the sewers into the daylight.[39]

The Russian President reacts strongly to minor foreign criticism of Russia, of what he considers the country's internal affairs, even on insignificant issues. For example, he responded to a criticism of *The New York Times* and many bloggers of "stacking" the World University Games in July 2013 with 18 London Olympic gold-medal winners, with a suggestion that the critics should take Viagra, which would "improve their lives and unfold some of its bright sides."[40]

THE NORTH CAUCASUS: NO ROOM FOR COMPROMISE

There is no room for compromise in the North Caucasus conflict. The Russian Empire and later the USSR subjugated the region with extreme brutality, and the local populace resisted with the same ferocity. Today's fighters for the freedom of North Caucasus battle for sovereignty and radical Islam. The region has long suffered from attacks. Colonel General Sergei Chenchik, Chief of the Main Directorate of the MVD of the Caucasus Federal Region, announced in January 2013 that in 2012, terrorists killed 211 members of the law enforcement organs and injured 405; 78 civilians were killed, and 179 were injured. The terrorists operate in smaller groups than previously and target members of security structures, public figures, religious leaders, and opposing extremists and terrorists. They also demand extortion money from local businessmen. In 2012, the Russian power structures killed 391 terrorists.[41]

During his visit to the HQ of the FSB in February 2013, President Putin announced that 99 crimes of a terrorist nature, including six specific terrorist acts, were prevented in 2012 but acknowledged the general "tense operational situation."[42] The unquestionable successes are overshadowed by the unchanging number of terrorist attacks. According to the MVD and General Prosecutor's Office, 295 terrorist crimes were committed in 2012 in Dagestan alone—more than in 2011. The number of crimes committed by armed groups in the first several months of 2013 was more than 100, and one-fifth of the 180 victims were civilians.[43]

The attacks on the Russian military decreased dramatically, as there were fewer of them and they were less involved in anti-terrorist operations. In 2012, attacks on the military and military bases represented up to 4 percent of all terrorist incidents. The local government institutions and law enforcement bodies became the priority target for the militants.[44] The official or semi-official upbeat announcements about terrorism in North Caucasus do not reflect the real situation. In August 2013, Ramzan Kadyrov, the Chechen leader, announced that there were 35 to 40 terrorists in Chechnya. He claimed that they recruit now weak-willed and mentally retarded young people.[45] No one believes him.

The FSB and the MVD forces in North Caucasus are quite clearly not sufficient to subdue the terrorists without major losses. Magomed Shamilov, Chairman of the Dagestani Independent Trade Union of Police Officers, wrote a letter to the national leadership reporting "steady and methodical extermination of police officers in the republic." According to Shamilov, in the recent years, more than 800 members of the MVD

died, and thousands were injured. In 2011, 188 policemen were killed in Dagestan, representing 50 percent
of the national police killings for that year.[46]

The conscription system has practically been abolished in the region. Only 179 young Dagestanis were
drafted in 2012, and only 42 of them were to serve in
the Russian MO. The rest serve in the Emergency Situations Ministry. Until 2010, every year 15,000-20,000
young men were drafted in the republic, but only
2,009 were drafted in 2011. Conscription in Dagestan
was stopped, because the draftees from that region
are usually undisciplined and intolerant of other eth-
nic groups. The Russian authorities worry also that
the conscripts serve as an information source for the
terrorists, and that their military training is used by
criminals and terrorists.[47]

The second biggest problem after terrorism in
North Caucasus is unemployment. At the beginning
of July 2010 at a meeting in Kislovodsk, Russia, Putin
announced new economic plans to improve the situation, but admitted at the same time how much room
for improvement there is in the region. In Ingushetia,
Russia, 50 percent of the working population was
unemployed; in Chechnya, the number is 30 percent.
At the very end of his speech, the Russian President
asked, "What must be done to stop corruption in the
region? He suggested hanging, but then added, "but
this is not our method."[48] Acting President of Dagestan Ramazan Abdulatipov said in May 2013 that terrorism is the result of long-term lawlessness and corruption of the local authorities. He argued that there
is nothing new in these attacks — this is a continuation
of age-old policies and fanaticism, and the failure
to implement promised social and economic plans.
Abdulatipov claims that:

even as an amateur, I am convinced that there is a clear operational, spying, and intelligence work, a lot of random people got jobs in the law enforcement organs of Dagestan through connections, not on merit.[49]

In July, Abdulatipov said that the new wave of terrorist attacks was the answer to the purge of the municipal bad apples ordered by the federal authorities.[50]

Aleksey Alekseevich Grishin, a former security officer and a present member of the Russian Duma, argues that the ineffective work of the special services in the region is a problem of unqualified and untrained personnel — only about 10 percent of those operating against radical Islamic groups are properly trained. A former security service officer and a member of the Public Council of the FSB, Lieutenant General (Rs) Andrey Stanislavovich Przhzdomskiy added that the local authorities in Dagestan do not conduct a sufficiently robust information and propaganda campaign in the republic.[51] In Spring 2013, the terrorists began to target the personnel of the Russian power structures and teachers. The campaign covers Dagestan, Ingushetia, and Chechnya.[52] In July 2013, Timur Aliev of the *Rossiskaya Gazeta*, the government official daily, wrote, "The July 2013 killings, in Dagestan, of police officers, journalists, businessmen, and civilians happened one after the other."[53] On December 5, 2012, an employee of the TV & Radio Company was killed in Kabardino Balkaria, Russia. In February, several broadcasters of the station were threatened by militants. Various unspecified militant websites began to threaten journalists working in the region, and on December 1, 2012, one of the Dagestani extremists published "a warning to journalists" that they, together with the members of special forces, the military, and government officials became the priority target. The message made it clear that a list of potential victims was already being compiled.[54] The most successful terrorist killing campaign is against "disobedient" imams in the whole of Russia. Indeed, the elimination of "disobedient" imams across Russia shows clearly a long-term strategy of the militants and the inability of the Russian state to take appropriate action.

In October 2012, Russian military units began to return to North Caucasus to participate in anti-terrorist operations. They closely cooperate with the FSB and MVD organs. This is partly to help suppress the unrelenting terrorist campaign and partly to gain experience before the Winter Olympics in Sochi, Russia, and to learn how to synchronize their actions with other security actors in the region. The communications networks of the power structures in North Caucasus are still not compatible, although special communications links were introduced recently.[55]

The Russian General Staff officials and the Military Intelligence Directorate (GRU) have asked Russian Minister of Defense Sergei Shoigu to create a Special Operations Command, with the Special Forces center—which would be answerable only to the Defence Minister. It would include a Special Forces brigade "borrowed" from one of the military districts, a helicopter squadron, and a squadron of transport Il-76s. The command would undertake special missions such as freeing hostages on enemy territory, evacuating citizens from local conflict zones, and liquidating terrorist formations. During a war, the command would be responsible for eliminating enemy leadership, strategic sites, communication hubs, nuclear missile launch facilities, and so on. A similar project was rejected by Shoigu's predecessor.[56]

The Russian federal and local security and law enforcement organs appear to concentrate their efforts in three principal directions:

1. Killing or arresting of terrorists. In a shootout with the federal forces, the terrorists practically never surrender.

2. Combating corruption—a particularly difficult task considering the old customs, clan and family links at every level, economic poverty and high unemployment, the high level of corruption everywhere in Russia, and terrorist intimidations.

3. Eliminating terrorist "tax collectors." The "collectors" are less visible than the terrorist fighters organizing explosions and killings but equally deadly when surrounded.

Although they occasionally lose their officers and troops in shootouts, the federal forces are not unsuccessful in eliminating terrorists. Never very subtle, they blow up the houses of terrorists when they find explosives in them, arguing that it is done for security reasons. The residents of these houses argue in return that the explosive are planted by the Russian forces. Six houses which belonged to the militants were blown up in April 2013 in Gimry village in Dagestan. According to the National Anti-terrorist Committee, improvised explosive devices (IEDs) were found in each of them, and sappers managed to neutralize them only with assistance of special charges.[57]

Russian anti-terrorist units are increasingly better trained and better equipped for their missions. During 16 anti-terrorist operations in July/August 2013, they killed 43 terrorists — according to the information released by the NAC, the terrorists refused to surrender — and arrested two terrorists.

At the same time, the Russian authorities are conducting a countercorruption campaign. In April 2013, the head of the government of the Republic of Ingushetia, Musa Chiliev, was investigated for paying $1 million of "protection" money to terrorists. The investigation was conducted by General Prosecutor Yury Chaika.[58] This is a particularly demanding campaign, as both sides in this type of corruption deal have very little interest in cooperating with the federal authorities, since losing, in many cases, means death for both those who cooperate — who are killed by terrorists — and for terrorists, who are killed by the Russian special forces. A group of the terrorist "tax collectors" was eliminated in March 2013. The leader of the "collectors," Ibragim Gadzhidadaev, was credited with forcing almost half of the businessmen in Dagestan to pay "taxes." The gang killed about 30 people. One of the five killed militants was the chairman of the Assembly of Untsukulsky Distric, Magomedkhabib Magomedaliev.[59]

Anti-terrorist operations are not made easier by a territorial dispute between Chechnya and Ingushetia, after the Chechen parliament passed a bill in March 2013 on the inclusion of the Ingush Sunzha District in Chechnya. When a group of armed Chechens crossed the administrative border between Chechnya and Ingushetia, they were stopped by the local police. The Ingush claimed that the Chechens wanted to organize a political meeting in support of their territorial claim. The Chechen leader argued that the Ingush policemen ruined a special operation to catch Russia's most wanted terrorist, Doku Umarov.[60]

SOCHI: THE TOP PRIORITY

The Winter Olympic Games in Sochi in 2014 will be a vital test for the Russian security and law enforcement organizations. The North Caucasian militants and their allies will do everything they can to disrupt it. Doku Umarov, the leader of the Chechen radicals appealed in July 2013 to his supporters to use "any methods" to disrupt the games, which he called the "satanic dances on the bones of our ancestors," in reference to the many Circassians killed by Russian troops in the Sochi area in the 19th century.[61]

The recent deadly terrorist attacks in North Caucasus indicate that the Russian security forces are not in control of the region, and that time is not on their side. During the games, security is bound to be extremely tight, bordering on oppressive, which will guarantee instant criticism from some sections of the foreign media and politicians. If the Russian security system succeeds in keeping the security lid on and preventing explosions and attacks, the strict security measures will be forgiven, remembered, and learned. If they fail, the consequences can be very serious, depending on the scale of the failure and possible foreign connections of the perpetrators. Russia would pursue them at home and abroad with the same determination the United States pursues their "most wanted," and with even less subtlety, and the relations with the countries which are seen in Moscow as protectors of terrorists could become very complicated irrespective of Russia's economic and political interests.

During the games, there will be a defense perimeter along the state borders of Abkhazia and the administrative borders with Kabardino Balkaria. Army special forces are going to cover the southern part of the

Krasnodar region and Karachevo-Cherkessiya. This is an order given to the Operational Group "Sochi" set up in August 2012. Army special forces will also patrol the mountainous regions close to Sochi. On the border with Georgia, they will be supported by units of the 58th Army. The group "Sochi" includes the 22nd Special Forces Brigade, located in the Stepnoye Pole village, and the 10th Brigade relocated to Gory-achi Klyuch village in the Krasnodar region. These are the two best mountain units in the Russian Army. The aviation of the operational group will be based in Korenovsk (Kuban), Budeyonnovsk, and Stavropol. If it is true that a third Special Forces Brigade is to be formed in Yessentukhi, the total number of special forces soldiers and officers will be more than 10,000.[62]

According to a paper produced for the Commercial Real Estate Broker, Cushman and Wakefield, by their Moscow office, Sochi can expect between 200,000 and 300,000 visitors during the games.[63] The games are expected to be attended by more than 15,000 U.S. fans — not counting the customers of the sponsoring companies.[64] One of the Russian commentators remarked that the Kremlin "returned" to Dagestan for the sake of the security of the Olympics, and his description of the problems in the area indicates that it left much too soon.[65]

THE TEPID PEACE: THE CONTEXT OF THE U.S.-RUSSIA RELATIONSHIP

Irrespective of the security requirements of the United States and Russia, close anti-terrorist cooperation between the two countries is going to be troubled by political disputes. Moscow rejects any sense of what it sees as U.S. interference in Russian domestic affairs. The list of U.S. concerns about Russian domestic policies, however, is lengthy, and includes the curtailed freedom of public rallies and nongovernmental organizations (NGOs), criminal punishment for libel, the "black list" of Internet sites, and the prohibition of "propaganda" relating to homosexuality. Nothing damages the relationship between the United States and Russia as much as Washington's criticism of what Moscow considers to be its internal affairs. Similarly, the Russian leadership regards the U.S. public support given to the controversial opposition activist, Aleksey Navalny, by the U.S. ambassador in Moscow, after Navalny was sentenced to 5 years in a penal colony for embezzling 16 million rubles (£330,000) from a state-owned timber company, as a further instance of U.S. interference in Russian domestic affairs.[66]

Another point of contention is the Magnitsky Act, passed by the U.S. Congress at the end of 2012 named after Sergey Magnitsky, a lawyer who died in a Moscow prison in 2009. Although the U.S. interest in the case was understandable because Sergey Magnitsky investigated an alleged crime for London-based Capital Heritage Management, set up by a U.S. national, the Act named after him was bound to provoke a tit-for-tat reaction. It allows the United States to withhold visas and freeze financial assets of Russian officials thought to have been involved with human rights violations.[67] The list of 18 people made public by U.S. authorities includes at least two individuals not involved in the Magnitsky case.[68] Russia retaliated with a similar list known in Russia as the Dmitri Yakovlev bill. On April 13, 2013, Russia released the list naming 18 Americans banned from entering the Russian Federation over their alleged human rights violations.[69]

However, the event which may have most significantly damaged U.S.-Russia anti-terrorist cooperation was the case of Ryan Fogle, an alleged Central Intelligence Agency (CIA) officer who was arrested by the FSB when he tried to recruit an FSB officer. The Russians were particularly annoyed because a request in October 2011 to the CIA station chief in Moscow to stop recruiting attempts of Russian intelligence agents went apparently unheeded.[70] The FSB showed the Americans not only the names of the alleged recruiters but also their Russian "targets." On January 11, 2013, the FSB detained an alleged CIA agent who attempted to recruit a member of the Russian NAC. The detained man was expelled from Russia the following month. The Russians were particularly angry because the NAC works closely with U.S. law enforcement agencies, and both Russian officers appear to have been known to the Americans as anti-terrorist operators after Moscow assisted the United States in the investigation of the Boston bombers.[71] If that is indeed the case, the anti-terrorist cooperation between the countries will be quite complicated and the effects of the alleged recruitment attempt—understandable operationally but imprudent politically—could last for years.

The relations between the two countries deteriorated still further on July 31, 2013, when U.S. National Security Agency (NSA) contractor Edward Snowden was granted temporary asylum in Russia.[72] Arrogant, badly organized, and in pursuit of the lime-light, Snowden painted himself into a corner reserved for traitors and defectors. He was preoccupied with his mission and his own importance just like Bernon F. Mitchell and William H. Martin, two NSA employees who defected to the USSR 53 years earlier.[73] The U.S.

anger at the Russian government was understandable; its surprise is not. No Soviet or Russian defectors were ever sent back to Moscow, although one or two returned voluntarily. There is also no doubt that the United States would not have sent back any Russian security defectors, if requested to do so by Moscow. The Russians asked the United States to extradite Ilyas Akhmadov, a former public affairs officer to Aslan Maskhadov, who was granted asylum in the United States in 2004, in spite of objections from the U.S. Department of Homeland Security. (He was, however, supported by some members of the U.S. Congress.) He is currently a Reagan-Fascell Democracy Fellow at the National Endowment for Democracy in Washington, DC.[74] The Russians argue that between 2011 and 2012, the United States did not answer five Russian extradition requests. Deputy Russian Prosecutor General Alexander Zvyagintsev, said that "since 2008, the United States has refused 16 times to extradite people to us, citing the absence of a relevant treaty."[75]

Referring to the Snowden case, President Barack Obama was reported as saying:

> I think the latest episode is just one more in a number of emerging differences that we've seen over the last several months around Syria, around human rights issues where, you know, it is probably appropriate for us to take a pause, reassess where it is that Russia is going, what our core interests are, and calibrate the relationship so that we're doing things that are good for the United States and, hopefully, good for Russia.[76]

The Snowden case has served as a catalyst for U.S. reaction. Due to the issue, President Obama cancelled his meeting with President Putin in Moscow.[77]

Yuriy Ushakov, Putin's top foreign policy adviser, announced that Moscow was disappointed, adding that:

> It is clear that this decision has been prompted by the situation regarding former U.S. spy agency employee, Edward Snowden, [a situation] which was not created by us.[78]

He also commented that the Snowden case shows the United States does not see Russia as an equal partner.[79] Vladimir Batyuk—the head of the Military-Political Research Centre of the U.S.-Canada Institute—remarked that if Obama did not plan to meet the Russian leader, that would be evidence that there is nothing special to be signed. Alexei Pushkov, the head of the International Committee of the State Duma, suggested that the reaction to Obama's decision should be calm, and that a meeting of the two leaders would be appropriate just now, so the old problems could be resolved, and a new agenda determined. His first deputy, Leonid Kalashnikov—a member of the Communist Party—added "Obama has done so under duress, as he did when he signed the Magnitsky law. . . . Americans in this situation are losing much more than the Russians." Sergey Neverov, Secretary of the General Council of "United Russia," added that the United States is the main loser because of Obama's decision.[80] By refusing to meet with Putin, Obama has not achieved anything. Washington may pick and choose when it wants to talk to Moscow, but in return, Moscow will choose when it wants to listen and cooperate. It is difficult to imagine that anyone in Washington could expect that this decision, announced publicly, would change any Russian policy. An unnamed Russian diplomatic source said:

Obama turned to personalities, which was absolutely unacceptable. He said that it was necessary to watch development of the situation in Russia. What is there to watch? He would better come and talk to us.[81]

The Russians are also convinced that President Obama is "specially pre-prepared" on Russian issues.[82] President Obama's decision not to go to Moscow not only looks like double standards — the United States would have done exactly the same with a Russian national claiming, for the same reason, asylum in the United States — but achieved nothing.

The decision not to go to Moscow before the G-20 summit stopped also an initiative taken by President Obama when, on April 15, 2013, he sent a message to his Russian counterpart, delivered by Tom Donilon, the U.S. national security adviser, arguing that the United States and Russia are two great powers with a special historical mission and must work together to solve global problems, and not to quarrel over trifles.[83] President Obama offered economic and political cooperation, including issues of strategic stability, terrorism, missile defense, and Syria.[84] It was well received in Moscow, although Ushakov remarked that Obama has not done anything to reduce the "Russophobia" in unspecified parts of the American government, by which he probably meant Congress.[85]

Putin's answer was delivered to the White House on May 22, 2013, by Nikolay Patrushev, the Secretary of the Russian Security Council, and one of Putin's closest and oldest colleagues and subordinates. Patrushev met Donilon and the U.S. President briefly joined in the discussion.[86] Patrushev found his trip very productive and, according to him, his meeting with Obama was of a profound nature and content, and he expressed hope that the talks on the subjects dividing the two sides would continue.[87]

But with Edward Snowden landing in Moscow, on June 23, 2013, the dialogue between the two countries practically stopped. The visit to Washington, DC, by Foreign Minister Lavrov and Defence Minister Sergey Shoigu at the beginning of August was low key and has not achieved anything, although Lavrov stated that Russia and the United States agree on several points. Both ministers wanted to show that there was no crisis in relations between the countries. Lavrov stated that Russia and the United States had similar positions on several issues, such as Afghanistan (preserving of stability in the country after the withdrawal of the International Security Assistance Force, Syria (the postponed Geneva-2 conference), the Iranian nuclear program (the need to organize the postponed meeting of the "Iranian six" which would address the Iranian nuclear challenges), combating the proliferation of weapons of mass destruction, and cooperation on the outer space program, among others. However, with Snowden loitering in Russia, the United States downplayed the visit of the two ministers as much as it was diplomatically possible, missing an opportunity to continue several parallel dialogs on the issues dividing the two countries.[88]

SYRIA, IRAN, AFGHANISTAN AND NATO MISSILE DEFENSE – PROBLEMS OR CHALLENGES?

The disagreements between the two countries in the international arena appear to be based on two fundamental preconceptions: the U.S. conviction that Russia would become a "proper" democracy if only

Putin and people close to him either accepted criticism coming from Washington and some European capitals (or disappeared altogether), and the Russian annoyance and surprise that Washington still does what it has been doing for the last 2 decades, criticizing publicly Russia's internal affairs. The issues dividing the United States and Russia reflect two simple realities:

1. The United States can do whatever it wishes to do, but should expect Russia to be very awkward, unless such help serves Moscow's interests as well.

2. If U.S. actions are seen to damage Russia's interests, Moscow will do everything, short of military intervention, to stop or disrupt them, irrespective how unethical the Russian response may look in Washington.

Syria.

Russia is unlikely to change its position on Syria as long as it believes that Bashar Assad may win the conflict. If the opposition wins, Moscow will lose its only ally in the region and will suffer serious financial loses. As long as there is a glimmer of hope that Assad could survive, Moscow will do everything to help him. If Assad loses, Russia's position in the Middle East will be similar to that of the USSR in the mid-1950s.

Iran.

Putin's visit to Teheran in October 2007 was the first visit of a Soviet/Russian leader since 1943. Russia has no major problems with the rulers in Teheran and much to gain from a good relationship with them. If Assad falls, Moscow may even try to strengthen its ties with Iran and sponsor robustly Iran's membership in the Shanghai Cooperation Organization (SCO).

Afghanistan.

Nikolay Patrushev, Secretary of the Russian Security Council, said after his visit to Washington that the Taliban's top leadership is not interested in serious peace talks because they aim to control most of Afghanistan after 2014.[89] On the one hand, Moscow has watched with some degree of satisfaction as NATO has failed to democratize Afghanistan. On the other, if the Taliban take over Afghanistan and implement their previous policies, Tajikistan and other Central Asian countries would be the first targets of radicalism originating in Kabul. The cooperation between the United States, Russia, and the regional countries could become a success, providing that Washington does not attempt to dominate the region and publicly lecture its potential partners.

NATO Missile Defense.

The NATO anti-missile defense program is probably the most straightforward issue dividing the two countries. As long as Moscow feels that the new system undermines its nuclear forces and damages the nuclear parity with the United States, it will do everything to keep this balance intact, deploying its missiles when it deems necessary. Washington's attempts to convince Moscow that the new system is supposed to protect the West from attacks from Iran and/or North Korea failed to convince anyone in Russia.

Numerous foreign policy differences between Russia and the West are something Moscow is prepared for and deals with calmly and diplomatically. During his almost annual TV appearance on "Direct Line" at the end of April 2013, Putin said that:

> some cooling in our relations began with events in Iraq. It began not yesterday, not last year and not this year. Then events in Libya and other parts of the world began. . . . We observe chaos everywhere. And we do not think that our partners' position is absolutely right.[90]

CONCLUSIONS

The principal, if not the only, strategic decision-maker in the Russian Federation is President Putin. He is a popular leader, and even those critical of him have difficulty finding a credible political personality, in the eyes of the Russian voter, who could challenge him. Strong criticism of Putin by a segment of Moscow and St. Petersburg intellectuals and middle classes, supported by many respected and vocal individuals and journalist in the United States and Europe, helped to create an illusion that Russia is full of potentially competent liberal democrats. But this is not the case, and barring an unexpected incident or illness, Putin is going to be in charge for many years. How well Western leaders will be able to cooperate with Russia depends partly on whether they will be willing to tone-down their public criticism of Russian internal policies, and Putin in particular. Moscow rightly accuses the West of double standards as its criticism is never directed at some of the far more deserving and much less transparent countries. Russia complained vociferously about these double standards on several occasions in the recent past.[91]

President Putin sees the international issues as things which can be discussed, but Russia's internal affairs are not. Anything seen in Moscow as a public attempt to "democratize" Russia will be instantly and uncompromisingly rejected by Russian leaders. This kind of public criticism may win some support on the domestic political arena in the West and please a large section of the media but will achieve nothing, except further damaging relations with Moscow. The decision of President Obama not to meet Putin before the G-20 summit met with little comprehension in Russia, especially because it was made a day after he expressed his disappointment about the Russians giving Edward Snowden a temporary refuge.[92]

At another level, there is a gap between Russia and the United States in terms of priorities regarding terrorism. The theory that the United States needs Russia more than Russia needs the United States may have been the case before the Winter Olympic Games in Sochi. The uncompromising Islamic radicals in Russia will do everything they can to disrupt the Games either by attacking the event directly, or conducting a bloody and spectacular attack in Russia which would overshadow the games. For Moscow, this is the primary terrorist challenge. Russian forces may win the war against the radicals at Sochi, but they are not anywhere near winning the continuing anti-terrorist campaigns. The slow, partially successful anti-terrorist campaign in the North Caucasus, the oppressive regime in Chechnya, and the comparatively generous benefits offered to all refugees in Europe, especially in Germany, may bring another danger if the terrorist attacks in Russia continue. Europe, especially Germany, faces a wave of Chechen refugees. In the first 7 months of 2013, more than 10,000 Chechens applied for asylum in Germany, almost three times as many as in all of 2012.[93] The generous German package for refugees — if they are accepted — attracted asylum claimers, including Chechens, from other countries. For example, between 2008 and 2009, Poland accepted more than 3,000 Chechens for either asylum status or "subsidiary protection." However, since then, the number of Chechens offered protected status in Poland dropped to fewer than 600 between 2010 and 2013.[94] The integration of that group, irrespective of how many claimants will be accepted, will not be easy. The case of the Tsarnayev brothers (the Boston Marathon bombers) and the arrest of the three Chechens in France in March 2013 shows that a small minority of the Chechen diaspora in democratic countries are vulnerable targets for radical recruiters and will continue waging their battles from the countries which offered them asylum.[95] Any terrorist attacks in Russia, or Russian interests abroad organized in Western democracies, are bound to create tension between Russia and these countries. As the political and legal constraints exclude sending the alleged terrorist suspects back to Russia, especially from Europe, the less than easy relationship between Moscow and most of the Western capitals may become very tense if the Sochi games are disrupted by terrorist attacks planned in democratic countries.

In a world addicted to media appearances and instant sound bites, it is very difficult to convince our democratically elected leaders that a quiet, long-term diplomacy built on in-depth knowledge of the subject, the countries they deal with, and patience is an attractive option which could achieve the successes which may happened in a distant future when they are not in charge. Toning down the top level criticism of Russia and replacing it with quiet diplomacy would be a very important and positive step towards improving relations between Russian and its Western partners, especially the United States.

The issues dividing the United States and Russia should not be fused and presented as a set of problems which have to be addressed together. Everything or nothing—large package deals will not achieve much, simply because mutual trust must be restored gradually. Large strategic issues can be repacked into individual issues and then addressed separately. The failure to reach agreement should not provoke a chain reaction of public criticism and recriminations. The economic, cultural, or educational cooperation between Russia and the liberal democracies will be driven largely by the supply and demand factor. No amount of successful economic or cultural cooperation will improve security cooperation between the two countries if the present political tension between the United States and Russia continues. Counterterrorism cooperation requires a thoughtful, well planned, step-by-step approach, not media-pleasing performances aimed exclusively at Western audiences.[96] Anyone expecting to share with Russia common democratic values in the near future will have to wait for a long time.

ENDNOTES

1. Vasiliy Mitrokhin, *KGB Lexicon*, London, UK: Frank Cass, 2002, p. 393.

2. Major General (KGB) Vadim Nikolayevich Udilov, *Terakty i Diversiy v SSSR. Stoprotsentnaya Raskryvaemost* (*Terrorist Acts and Sabotage in the USSR. A Hundred Percent Clear-up Rate*), Moscow, Russia: Eksmo Algoritm, 2011, p. 126.

3. *Ibid.*, p. 222.

4. *Ibid.*, pp. 222-223.

5. Dhokhar Dudayev, the Chechen leader, announced the independence of Chechnya on November 1, 1991. "Chechenskaya Tragedya. Kto Vinovat" ("The Chechen Tragedy. Who is to be blamed?"), *RIA Novosti*, 1995, p. 20.

6. In 1991, 4,500 crimes involving the use of firearms, ammunition, and explosives were committed in Russia. The following year, this number almost doubled, and in 1993, the number reached 19,100. In 1992, there were about 100 contract killings in Russia, which doubled the following year. V. E. Petrishchev, *Zametki o terrorizme* (*Notes on Terrorism*), Moscow, Russia: URSS, 2001, p. 26. Leonid Shebarshin, the former head of the KGB Intelligence Directorate, observed in one of his books that July 25, 1991, was an important date because for the first time in recent Soviet history, the F-1 hand grenade was used against the police. Leonid Shebarshin, *Khronika Bezvremenya. Zametki Byvshego Nachalnika Razvedki* (*Chronicles of Stagnation. Notes of the Former Head of the Intelligence Service*), Gagarina, Russia: Russkiy Biograficheskiy Institut, 1998, p. 24.

7. Gordon Bennett, *The Federal Security Service of the Russian Federation*, C102, Sandhurst, UK: Conflict Studies Research Centre, March 2000, p. 2, available from *www.da.mod.uk/colleges/arag/document-listings/russian/C106*.

8. For the reforms of and the power struggle within the Russian security sector and the law enforcement organs in the 1990s, see *Ibid.*; and also *www.agentura.ru/library/csrc/fsb.pdf*.

9. Petrishchev, p. 35.

10. A Soviet motor rifle division located in Chechnya in 1991 was staffed by less than 10 percent of the required personnel. *The Chechen Tragedy*, p. 20.

11. *Bratishka,* in Russian, January 2011, p. 79.

12. A.V. Vozhennikov, ed., *Mezhdunarodniy Terrorism* (*International Terrorism*), RAGS, 2005, p. 309, quoting *Musulmanskye dukhovye organizatsiy i obyedinenya*, in Russian, March 1999, p. 54; and *Tatarskye kraya,* in Russian, July 1997.

13. Vozhennikov, p. 310, quoting Yu. Anchabadze, "Kavkaz posle Novoy Chechenskoy Voiny" ("The Caucasus After The New Chechen War"), *Tsentr Strategicheskikh i Politicheskich Isledovaniy*, Byuleten Nr 1, p. 35.

14. Vozhennikov, pp. 301-340.

15. *"О внесении изменений и дополнений в Уголовный кодекс РСФСР и Уголовно-процессуальный кодекс РСФСР"* ("On introduction of amendments and supplements to the Criminal Code of the Russian Federation and the Criminal Procedure Code of the RSFSR"), available from *docs.cntd.ru/document/9006528;* and V. Ye. Petrushev, *Zametki o Terrorizme* (*Notes on Terrorism*), Moscow, Russia: URSS, 2001, p. 213. The old Criminal Code was superseded by the Criminal Code of 1996 and its supplements.

16. *Уголовный кодекс Российской Федерации от 13.06.1996 N 63-ФЗ (ред. от 23.07.2013)* (*The Criminal Code of the Russian Federation*), June 13, 1996, No. 63-FZ, (version as of July 23, 2013), Moscow, Russia, available from *www.ug-kodeks.ru/ug/ug-kodeks.ru/ugolovnij_kodeks_-_glava_24.html.*

17. Федеральный закон от 6 марта 2006 г. N 35-ФЗ "О противодействии терроризму" (The Federal Law N 35-ФЗ, "On Countering Terrorism"), available from the official website of the National Anti-terrorist Council, *nac.gov.ru/content/3888.html.*

18. *Ibid.*

19. *Федеральный закон Российской Федерации от 6 марта 2006 г. N 35-ФЗ О противодействии терроризму* (*The Federal Law of the Russian Federation "On Countering Terrorism" Nr 35-F3*), Moscow, Russia: March 6, 2006, available from *www.rg.ru/2006/03/10/borba-terrorizm.html.*

20. *Положение о Совете Безопасности Российской Федерации N 590* (*On the Security Council of the Russian Federation N 590*), The official site of the Security Council of the Russian Federation, Moscow, Russia: May 6, 2011, available from *www.scrf.gov.ru/documents/11/3.html.*

21. *Федеральный закон от 25 июля 1998 г. № 130-ФЗ* (*Federal law Nr 130-F3 of 25 July 1998 "On Combatting Terrorism"*), Moscow, Russia, available from *www.scrf.gov.ru/documents/17/30.html*.

22. The official site of the Russian Intelligence Service (SVR), available from *svr.gov.ru/svr_today/doc12.htm*.

23. *Ibid.*

24. The FSB, responsible for the internal security of Russia, "lost" its control over the intelligence operations, communications, cryptography, communications interception, and SIGINT.

25. *Федеральный закон Российской Федерации от 6 марта 2006 г. N 35-ФЗ О противодействии терроризму* (*The Federal Law of the Russian Federation of 6 March 2006, Nr 35-F3 On Countering Terrorism*), *Rossiskaya Gazeta*, March 10, 2006, available from *www.rg.ru/2006/03/10/borba-terrorizm.html*.

26. *Bratishka*, October 2011, p. 78; and July 2011, p. 78.

27. *Указ Президента Российской Федераций О мерах по протививодействию терроризму* (*Decree of the President of the Russian Federation on Measures Countering Terrorism, Nr 832s*), August 2, 2006, (with amendments), Moscow, Russia, available from *www.fsb.ru/fsb/npd/more.htm%21id%3D10342802%40fsbNpa.html*.

28. *Международное сотрудничество* (*The International Cooperation*), The FSB official website, available from *www.fsb.ru/fsb/international.html*.

29. Ivan Nechepurenko, "Russians to Get Access to FBI Data," *The Moscow Times*, May 27, 2013, available from *www.themoscowtimes.com/mobile/article/480497.html*.

30. Alexander Grigoriev, "ФБР заинтересовалось опытом борьбы России с терроризмом на Кавказе" ("The FBI Interested in the Experience of Combatting Terrorism in the Russian Caucasus"), *Izvestia*, May 27, 2013, available from *izvestia.ru/news/550957*.

31. Yury Paniev, "США и РФ поладят в киберпространстве" ("The US and the RF Will Get Along in Cyberspace"), *Nezavisimaya Gazeta*, May 16, 2013, available from *www.ng.ru/world/2013-05-16/1_rus_usa.html*.

32. "Moscow Safer Than New York — Minister," *RIA Novosti*, May 21, 2013, available from *en.rian.ru/world/20130521/181268611.html*.

33. The MVD official website, available from *mvd.ru/mvd/structure1/Glavnie_upravlenija/Glavnoe_upravlenie_po_protivodejstviju_j*.

34. The official site of the Internal Troops of the Ministry of Internal Affairs of the Russian Federation, available from *www.vvmvd.ru/menu2/structure/okruga/*.

35. The official site of the Internal Troops of the Ministry of Internal Affairs of the Russian Federation, available from *www.vvmvd.ru/menu2/structure/obishie/*.

36. BBC News, July 7, 2003, available from *news.bbc.co.uk/2/hi/europe/3050806.stm*; and RT Russiapedia, available from *russiapedia.rt.com/of-russian-origin/mochit-v-sortire/*.

37. Thomas Fuller, "Hint of Castrating Islamic Radicals Gets Lost in Translation: Putin's Words Spark Confusion at EU," *The New York Times*, November 13, 2002, available from *www.nytimes.com/2002/11/13/news/13iht-putin_ed3_.html*.

38. BBC News, July 7, 2003.

39. Archives of the site of Prime Minister V. V. Putin (in Russian), The Government of the Russian Federation official website, March 31, 2010, available from *archive.premier.gov.ru/premier/press/ru/4894/*; and Zhivoi Russkiy Yazyk, April 4, 2011, available from *skazanul.ru/slova/vykovyryat-so-dna-kanalizatsii*.

40. Andrew E. Kramer, "Russia Stacked Team with Stars for World University Games," *The New York Times*, July 17, 2013, available from *www.nytimes.com/2013/07/18/world/europe/russia-stacked-team-with-stars-for-world-university-games.html?_r=1&*; and Forbes (in Russian) Путин посоветовал «Виагру" критикам спортсменов

Универсиады (*Putin Advised His Critics to Take Viagra*), July 19, 2013, available from *www.forbes.ru/news/242410-putin-posovetoval-viagru-kritikam-sportsmenov-universiady*.

41. Vladimir Mukhin, "Бандподполье выходит из схронов" ("The Bandit Underground Leaves the Hideouts"), *Nezavisimaya Gazeta*, February 6, 2013, available from *www.ng.ru/regions/2013-02-06/1_caucasus.html*.

42. Kira Latukhina, "Экстремизм не пройдет" ("Extremism Will Not Pass"), *Rossiyskaya Gazeta*, February 15, 2013, available from *www.rg.ru/2013/02/14/zadachi-site.html*.

43. Vladimir Mukhin, "Армия боевиков пополняется "черными вдовами" ("Army Militants Reinforced By 'Black Widows'"), *Nezavisimaya Gazeta*, May 27, 2013, available from *www.ng.ru/regions/2013-05-27/1_boeviki.html*.

44. "Kirill Belyaninov, "Россию оставили под угрозой терроризма" ("Russia Was Left Under the Threat of Terrorism"), *Kommersant*, December 11, 2012, available from *www.Kommersant.ru/doc/2087374*.

45. *Argumenty I Fakty*, No. 43, October 24-30, 2012, available from *www.aif.ru/politics/article/56368*.

46. Vladimit Mukhin, "Третья чеченская война" ("The Third Chechen War"), *Nezavisimaya Gazeta*, October 10, 2012, available from *www.ng.ru/regions/2012-10-10/3_kartblansh.html*.

47. Denis Telmanov, "Вармию перестали брать дагестанцев" ("The Army Stopped Drafting Dagestanis"), *Izvestia*, October 11, 2012, available from *izvestia.ru/news/537309*.

48. Pierre Sidibe, "Вешать — не метод. Владимир Путин уверен, что побороть коррупцию сложнее, чем терроризм" ("Hanging is to the method. Vladimir Putin convinced that to fight corruption is more difficult than terrorism"), *Rossiskaya Gazeta*, July 7, 2013, available from *www.rg.ru/2010/07/07/putin.html*.

49. Vladimir Mukhin, "Армия боевиков пополняется ,черными вдовами'" ("Army militants reinforced by, 'black widows'"), *Nezavisimaya Gazeta*, May 27, 2013, available from *www.ng.ru/regions/2013-05-27/1_boeviki.html*.

50. Timur Aliev, "Пули без причин" ("Bullets For No Reason"), *Rossiskaya Gazeta*, July 17, 2013, available from *www.rg.ru/2013/07/17/ubiystvo.html*.

51. Mukhin, "Army militants reinforced by 'black widows'."

52. Vladimir Mukhin, "Боевики развернули минную войну" ("Militants Started a Mine Warfare"), *Nezavisimaya Gazeta*, April 5, 2013, available from *www.ng.ru/regions/2013-04-05/1_mines.html*; and Aliev, "Bullets For No Reason."

53. Aliev, "Bullets For No Reason."

54. Irina Gordyenko, "Боевики составили 'расстрельные списки'журналистов" ("Militants Composed 'hit lists' of Journalists"), *Novaya Gazeta*, December 6, 2012, available from *www.novayagazeta.ru/politics/55766.html?print=1*.

55. Elena Sidorenko, "Военное усиление" ("Military reinforcement"), *Vzglyad*, October 8, 2012, available from *vz.ru/society/2012/10/8/601538.html*.

56. Aleksey Mikhailov, "Генштаб просит Шойгу создать коммандос" ("The General Staff Asks Shoigu to Set Up a Special Command"), *Izvestia*, November 27, 2012, available from *izvestia.ru/news/540120#ixzz2DPoez8Vj*.

57. Yulya Rybina and Nikolay Sergeev, "Дома боевиков взрывают вместе с бомбами" ("Houses of Militants are Blown Up Together with Bombs"), *Kommersant*, May 8, 2013, available from *www.Kommersant.ru/doc/2185376*.

58. Anastasya Kashevarova, "Генпрокуратура проверит власти Ингушетии на связь с боевиками" ("Attorney General's Office Will Check the Ingush Authorities If They Have Contacts with Militants"), *Izvestia*, April 3, 2013, available from *izvestia.ru/news/547826*.

59. Sergey Mashkin and Nikolay Sergeev, "В Дагестане отменен налог на джихад" ("Jihad Tax Abolished in Dagestan), *Kommersant*, April 3, 2013, available from *www.Kommersant.ru/doc/2161306*.

60. Alexei Sokovnin and Sergei Mashkin , "Сход в режиме спецоперации" ("The Gathering in the Special Operations Mode"), *Kommersant*, April 20, 2013, available from *www.Kommersant.ru/doc/2175699*.

61. Tom Parfitt, "Doku Umarov Calls for Islamists to Disrupt Sochi Winter Olympics," *The Telegraph*, July 3, 2013, available from *www.telegraph.co.uk/news/worldnews/europe/russia/10157474/Doku-Umarov-calls-for-Islamists-to-disrupt-Sochi-Winter-Olympics.html*.

62. Aleksey Mikhailov, "К защите Олимпиады в Сочи подключился армейский спецназ" ("Army Special Forces Joins To Protect the Olympic Games in Sochi"), *Izvestia*, February 26, 2013, available from *izvestia.ru/news/543324*.

63. Sergey Riabokonylko and Co, *Sochi: The Impact of the 2014 Olympics*, Moscow, Russia: Cushman and Wakefield, p. 4; Stiles and Riabokobylko, "Sochi: The Impact of the 2014 Olympics," *1rre.ru*, October 20, 2013, p. 4, available from *www.1rre.ru/upload/iblock/330/analitics-realty-15122009-8.pdf*.

64. Alexander Grigoriev, "ФБР заинтересовалось опытом борьбы России с терроризмом на Кавказе" ("The FBI interested in the experience of combatting terrorism in the Russian Caucasus"), *Izvestia*, May 27, 2013, available from *izvestia.ru/news/550957*.

65. Milrad Fatullaev, "Кремль вернулся в Дагестан ради Олимпиады" ("The Kremlin Returned to Dagestan for the Sake of Olympics"), *Nezavisimaya Gazeta*, available from *www.ng.ru/regions/2013-06-11/5_dagestan.html*.

66. Sarah Yasin, "US and UK condemn Navalny conviction," *Index on Censorship*, July 18, 2013, available from *www.indexoncensorship.org/2013/07/russian-opposition-leader-sentenced-to-five-years-in-penal-colony/*.

67. "Q&A: The Magnitsky Affair," *BBC News Europe*, July 11, 2013, available from *www.bbc.co.uk/news/world-europe-20626960*.

68. Susan Cornwell, "U.S. names 18 people as alleged human rights abusers in Russia," *Reuters*, April 12, 2013, available from *www.reuters.com/article/2013/04/12/us-russia-usa-rights-idUS-BRE93B0PU20130412*.

69. David Hershenhorn and Andrew E. Kramer, *Russian Adoption Ban Brings Uncertainty and Outrage and RT Question More*, April 13, 2013, available from *rt.com/news/anti-magnitsky-list-russia-799/*.

70. Carl Schreck, "'Unprecedented' CIA Moscow Chief Leak Puzzles Ex-Spies," *RIA Novosti*, May 18, 2013, available from *en.rian.ru/russia/20130518/181212155/Unprecedented-CIA-Moscow--Chief-Leak-Puzzles-Ex-Spies.html*.

71. Perviy Kanal TV, in Russian, May 17, 2013. The Russians were somewhat selective in their outrage as their own spying activities have not diminished since the collapse of the USSR.

72. "Free in Russia: Whistleblower Snowden Leaves Moscow Airport," *Spiegel Online International*, August 1, 2013, available from *www.spiegel.de/international/world/whistleblower-snow den-leaves-moscow-airport-a-914332.html*.

73. Wayne G. Barker and Rodney E. Coffman, *The Anatomy of Two Traitors. The Defection of Bernon F. Mitchell and William H. Martin*, Walnut Creek, CA: Aegean Park Press, 1981.

74. "A Chechnya Plan: Talk by Ilyas Akhmadov," *The Washington Post*, December 10, 2004, available from *www.washing-tonpost.com/wp-dyn/articles/A53778-2004Dec9.html*; and "Political groups in Washington downplayed Chechen threat," RT, April 22, 2013, available from *rt.com/op-edge/washington-downplayed-chechen-threat-213/*.

75. "US Left 5 Extradition Requests Unanswered—Russia," *RIA Novosti*, July 21, 2013, available from *en.ria.ru/politics/20130821/182880299/US-Left-5-Extradition-Requests-Unanswered---Russia.html*.

76. "Barack Obama: US to 'take a pause' in relationship with Russia," ITV News, August 9, 2013, available from *www.itv.com/news/2013-08-09/barack-obama-us-to-take-a-pause-in-relationship--with-russia/*.

77. Peter Baker and Steven Lee Myers, "Ties Fraying, Obama Drops Putin Meeting," *The New York Times*, August 7, 2013, available from *www.nytimes.com/2013/08/08/world/europe/obama-cancels-visit-to-putin-as-snowden-adds-to-tensions.html?pagewanted=all*.

78. "Kremlin 'Disappointed' That Obama's Visit to Moscow Is Canceled," *RIA Novosti*, August 7, 2013, available from *en.rian.ru/russia/20130807/182633034.html*.

79. "Обама отменил встречу с Путиным" ("Obama cancelled a meeting with Putin"), *RIA Novosti*, August 7, 2013, available from *ria.ru/world/20130807/954907949.html*.

80. "Эксперты об отмене визита Обамы: американцы пострадают больше, чем мы" ("Experts comment on the cancellation of Obama's visit: Americans will lose more than we do"), *RIA Novosti*, August 7, 2013, available from *ria.ru/politics/20130807/954944155.html*.

81. Pavel Tarasenko, Ivan Safronov, and Yelena Chernenko, "'Перезагрузку' поставили на паузу" ("The 'Reset' was Paused"), *Kommersant*, August 12, 2013, available from *www.Kommersant.ru/doc/2253581*.

82. *Ibid.*

83. Yelena Chernenko and Ivan Safronov, "Доверительные грамоты" ("Letters of Trust"), *Kommersant*, May 15, 2013, available from *www.Kommersant.ru/doc/2187951?isSearch=True*.

84. Eugenia Novikova, "Ответ Путина доставлен Обаме" ("Putin's Answer Has Been Delivered to Obama"),

Nezavisimaya Gazeta, May 24, 2013, available from *www.ng.ru/world/2013-05-24/8_obama.html*.

85. Will Englund, "Obama Letter to Putin Sends 'Positive Signals,' Russian Official Says"), *The Washington Post*, April 15, 2013, available from *articles.washingtonpost.com/2013-04-15/world/38548005_1_sergei-magnitsky-rule-law-accountability-act-positive-signals*.

86. Eugenia Novikova, "Ответ Путина доставлен Обаме" ("Putin's Answer Has Been Delivered to Obama"), *Nezavisimaya Gazeta*, May 24, 2013, available from *www.ng.ru/world/2013-05-24/8_obama.html*.

87. Pavel Koryashkin, "Предложения Барака Обамы идут в правильном направлении, но этого мало" ("Barack Obama's proposals go in the right direction, but this is not enough"), *Kommersant*, May 25, 2013, available from *www.Kommersant.ru/doc/2197826*.

88. Pavel Tarasenko, Ivan Safonov, and Yelena Chernenko, "'Перезагрузку' поставили на паузу" ("The 'Reset' was Paused"), *Kommersant*, August 12, 2013, available from *www.Kommersant.ru/doc/2253581*.

89. Pavel Koryashkin, "Предложения Барака Обамы идут в правильном направлении, но этого мало" ("Barack Obama's proposals go in the right direction, but this is not enough"), *Kommersant*, May 25, 2013, available from *www.Kommersant.ru/doc/2197826*.

90. Caitlin Dewey, "Putin's 9 most notable quotes from in his five-hour Q&A," *The Washington Post*, April 25, 2013, available from *www.washingtonpost.com/blogsworldviews/wp/2013/04/25/putins-9-most-notable-quotes-from-in-his-five-hour-qa/*.

91. Luke Harding, "Georgia: Moscow accuses west of double standards," *The Guardian*, August 30, 2008, available from *www.theguardian.com/world/2008/aug/30/russia.georgia*; "Moscow slams West's 'double standards'-based Syria policy," *Johnson's Russia*, July 9, 2013, quoting Interfax, July 8, 2013, available from *russialist.org/moscow-slams-wests-double-standards-based-syria-policy/*;

"Russian Minister Condemns West's 'Double Standards' on Syria," *RIA Novosti*, June 11, 2013, available from *en.rian.ru/russia/20130611/181611613.html*; Andrei Zolotov, "Moscow's Patriarch Accuses West of Double Standards Over Chechnya," *Christianity Today*, January 4, 2000, available from *www.christianitytoday.com/ct/2000/aprilweb-only/44.0a.html*; Jill Dohery, "Putin still sees double standard with West on terrorism," CNN, April 26, 2013, available from *security.blogs.cnn.com/2013/04/26/putin-still-sees-double-standard-with-west-on-terrorism/*.

92. Jay Leno's interview with President Obama (transcript, video), POLITICO, August 7, 2013, available from *www.politico.com/story/2013/08/jay-leno-obama-interview-transcript-video-95279.html#ixzz2dXgrl7B7*.

93. Benjamin Bidder and Maximilian Popp, "Third Wave: Thousands of Chechens Seek Refuge in Germany," *Der Spiegel Online*, in English, August 28, 2013, available from *www.spiegel.de/international/europe/refugees-from-chechnya-seek-new-life-in-germany-a-918720.html*.

94. Glenn Kates, "In Poland, Chechen Asylum Seekers Languish In Limbo," *Radio Free Europe/Radio Liberty*, August 14, 2013, available from *www.rferl.org/content/poland-chechnya-asylum-seekers-germany-limo/25075082.html*.

95. Al Goodman and Paul Cruickshank, CNN, March 1, 2013, available from *edition.cnn.com/2013/03/01/world/europe/france-terrorism-arrests*.

96. The "peregruzka" box that Secretary of State Hillary Clinton gave her Russian counterpart, Sergey Lavrov, on March 6, 2009, in Geneva, Switzerland, was not only badly translated but had no Russian (Cyrillic) writings.

APPENDIX I

THE RUSSIAN SECURITY PYRAMID

The Security Council.

The Security Council meets every 2 months, but the president meets the permanent members of the Council once a week to discuss operational issues or as often as the situation demands. The Council has the right to show interest in any aspect of the national security. The president has to approve the activities of every interdepartmental commission as well as its membership. The members of the Security Council are divided into 12 full voting members and 16 nonvoting members. The permanent (voting) members of the Council are usually the heads of the Russian power structures and politicians (as of August 2013):

Aleksandr Vasilevich BORTNIKOV	Director of the FSB
Boris Vyacheslavovich GRYZLOV	Full member of the Council
Sergey Borisovich IVANOV	Head of the Presidential Administration
Vladimir Aleksandorvich KOLOKOLTSEV	Minister of Internal Affairs
Sergey Viktorovich LAVROV	Minister of Foreign Affairs
Valentina Ivanovna MATEVEENKO	Chairperson of the Federation Council of the Federal Assembly
Dmitri Anatolyevich MEDVEDEV	Prime Minister
Sergey Yevgenevich NARYSHKIN	Chairman of the Duma of the Federal Assembly
Rashid Gumarovich NURGALIYEV	Deputy Secretary of the Security Council
Nikolay Platonovich PATRUSHEV	Secretary of the Security Council
Mikhail Yefimovich FRADKOV	Director of the Intelligence Service
Sergey Kuzhgetovich SHOIGU	Minister of Defence.

The National Anti-Terrorist Committee (NAC).

The NAC is divided into four principal structures:
1. The Directorate for the Coordination of the Anti-terrorist Preventive Actions is responsible for developing preventive measure against terrorism at the national level, including the relevant legal framework, protection of the population and the critical infrastructure, countermeasures against terrorist financial resources, eliminating and dealing with the effects of a terrorist act, and assisting their victims. This directorate is also responsible for the coordination and control of the regional anti-terrorist commissions in the Russian Federation and contacts with foreign organizations responsible for combating terrorism.
2. The Directorate for Intelligence and Internal Protection is responsible for anti-terrorist combat coordination and for operational matters and planning, anti-terrorist exercises and internal security.
3. The Information-Analytical Directorate, in addition to its main analytical work, has to develop and maintain its information systems and to implement the Federal Program "Anti-Terror 2009-2013."
4. The Information Center of the NAC deals with the media, psyops operations, and the organizational and information-analytical support for the operations of the Interagency Group responsible for information support of the NAC.

The final membership of the NAC was approved by Vladimir Putin on September 2, 2012. Members of the NAC include:
- Director of the Federal Security Service (FSB) — Chairman of the NAC.
- Minister of Internal Affairs (MVD) — Deputy Chairman.

- Deputy Director of the Russian Federal Security Service.
- Deputy Chairman — the Head of the Office of the NAC.
- Deputy Prime Minister of the Russian Federation — the Plenipotentiary Representative of the President of the Russian Federation in the North Caucasus Federal District.
- First Deputy Head of Presidential Administration of the Russian Federation.
- First Deputy Chairman of the Federation Council of the Federal Assembly of the Russian Federation.
- First Deputy Chairman of the State Duma of the Federal Assembly of the Russian Federation.
- Minister for Civil Defense, Emergencies and Elimination of Consequences of Natural Disasters.
- Minister of Foreign Affairs.
- Minister of Defence.
- Minister of Justice.
- Minister of Health.
- Minister of Industry and Trade.
- Minister of Communications and Mass Media.
- Minister of Transport.
- Minister of Power Industry.
- Director of the Intelligence Service.
- Director of the Federal Service for Control and Distribution of Drugs.
- Director of the Federal Guard Service.
- Director of the Financial Monitoring Service.
- Chief of Staff — First Deputy Minister of Defence.
- Deputy Secretary of the Security Council.

The NAC is divided into eight regional anti-terrorist commissions.

1. The Far Eastern Federal District.
2. The Volga Federal District.
3. The North-West Federal District.
4. The North-Caucasian Federal District.
5. The Siberian Federal District.
6. The Ural Federal District.
7. The Central Federal District.
8. The South Federal District.

The FSB.

The FSB consists of four principal parts supported by many supporting entities:

1. The central apparatus divided into services, departments, directorates and other subunits responsible for the management and implementation of its tasks on the territory of the Russian Federation.
2. The territorial organs (directorates and departments of the FSB in the regions).
3. Security and counter intelligence organs in the armed forces, the Ministry of Internal Affairs and other militarized organizations.
4. The Border Guards with its own aviation.

They share the supporting organs of the FSB:
- The aviation units.
- The scientific and research units.
- The educational establishments and centers.
- The expert and legal experts units.
- The special forces units.
- The military-medical units.

A CASE STUDY IN RUSSIAN DEALINGS WITH INTERNAL TERRORISM: CHECHNYA – HISTORY AND BLOODSHED

The Chechen population has never accepted Moscow's domination. To understand the difficulties facing the Russian law enforcement organs in North Caucasus, it should be remembered that Khasukha Magomedov, the most wanted criminal in the history of the region, was able to avoid arrest between 1939 and 1976. Between 1939 and 1951, Magomedov and the members of several groups he joined took part in 194 attacks, killing 33 Communist Party officials and security and police officers and injuring 10. After 1951, he began to operate on his own, assisted by the members of the local population. Magomedov was shot dead on March 28, 1976. According to the official Soviet sources, he had personally committed 30 murders. Many Chechen websites glorify Magomedov. Although those supporting him describe him as "arbek" a mountain fighter in loose translation, in reality he was a robber and killer.

Post-Soviet Chechnya became the hottest of Russia's potential hot spots. In November 1990, with the approval of the regional Communist Party, the National Council of the Chechen People was created. The Council became, de facto, a Chechen national party, but the Chechen leadership did not challenge the Russian Federation until the end of 1991. On November 1, 1991, Chechen leader Dzokhar Dudayev announced the sovereignty of Chechnya. Between 1991 and 1994, Dudayev had to fight his internal opponents—the conflict resembling more a war of mafias rather than a political struggle—and Moscow made an unsophisticated attempt to dislodge him. The first Chechen War began on December 11, 1994, when Russian troops, in three columns, moved towards the capital, Grozny. The first Chechen war ended in August 1996 and re-started 3 years later when Chechen radicals invaded Dagestan. The Russians responded with a large-scale military campaign. Ten years later, in April 2009, pro-Kremlin President Ramzan Kadyrov, announced that he was informed about the end of the anti-terrorist operation in Chechnya.

The militants, however, continued their unrelenting attacks. The *Global Terrorism Index 2012*, published by the Australian and the U.S. Institute of Economics and Peace, in 2011 listed Russia as the 9th among 115 countries affected by terrorism that year. In 2011, there were 187 terrorist incidents in Russia, with 159 people killed and 431 injured. Attacks on imams included:

- At the beginning of June 2010, a terrorist opened fire on the congregation of the mosque in the village of Tarki (Dagestan). Makhomed Kazakhbyev, the imam of the mosque, was killed, and several people were injured.
- Magomedvagif Sultanmagomedov, the head of the Islamic education department of the Islamic Religious Board of Dagestan, was killed on August 11, 2010 — the first day of Ramadan.
- The imam of the village Mikheevka (Dagestan), Ashurulav Kurbanov, was killed on November 6, 2011.
- Acting imam of the city of Ivanovo, Fuad Rustamkhodzhayev, was killed on September 24, 2011.
- Isomutdin Akbarov, an imam in Tyumen, was killed on October 10, 2011.

- Artur Manukyan, the second imam of the Yaroslav region principal mosque, was found dead on November 9, 2011. He was shot four times in front of his apartment.
- Gitinomagomed Abdulapurov, the imam of the Buinaksk (Dagestan) city mosque, and his bodyguard died on March 23, 2012, as a result of the explosion of an IED.
- Valiulla Yakupov, deputy mufti of Tatarstan, was killed in Kazan on July 19, 2012.
- Kalimulla Ibragimov, one of the imams of the town of Derbent, and two of his relatives were shot dead on October 30, 2012. The killing surprised the locals as the murdered imam belonged to a mosque supporting wahhabism. Ibragimov was not an official imam but his supporters regarded him as an imam.
- The imam of the village of Khadzalmakhi (Dagestan), Gadzhi Aliev, was shot dead on November 13, 2012. He was a known critic of the local extremists.
- Magomed Saipudinov, the imam of the Yasnaya Polana village of the Kizlyar region of Dagestan, was killed on April 9, 2013.
- On June 23, 2013, the imam of the Untsukul region of Dagestan shot dead one of the three attackers who tried to break into his house and kill him.
- Ilyas Khadzhi Ilyasov, the Imam of Alburikent (Dagestan), was murdered on August 4, 2013.

Counterterrorist operations in July-August 2013:
  — July 6: Three terrorists attacked a patrol car in Buinaksk. Two of them were killed and the third attacker escaped.

- July 8: One terrorist was killed after a shoot-out in Chechnya.
- July 12: Three terrorists died in a shootout in a village of Truzhennik.
- July 13: Two terrorist were shot dead in the village of Nesterovskoye, in Ingushetiya.
- July 13: A member of the Derbent terrorist group, Umar Musayev, was arrested after his house was surrounded by federal forces.
- July 18: Four militants were killed in the Bakinskiy region of Kabardino Balkaria.
- July 23: Two militants were killed after a shootout with the Federal forces in the Makhachkala region in Dagestan.
- July 27: Federal forces apprehended Yusup Kasymov in the village of Noviy Kostek of the Khasavyurt region. He resisted arrest and was killed after a brief firefight.
- July 30: The FSB arrested Ilmudin Kairbekov, the leader of the "Buynaksk" terrorist group.
- August 7: A team of traffic policemen shot and killed four militants in a fire-fight in Nalchik, the capital of Kabardino-Balkaria.
- August 11: Federal forces killed one militant near the station of Stalskoye in the Kizlyarskiy region of Dagestan. His companion escaped.
- August 17: Three militants were killed near the village of Manas.
- August 18: Six militants were eliminated in Khasavyurt by the FSB and MVD special forces.
- August 20: The Russian special forces killed nine terrorists, including their leader, Bammatkhan Sheikhov.

- August 28: Two terrorist were killed in a shootout near the village of Kvanda in Dagestan.
- August 30: Two terrorist were killed in two separate fire-fights in Dagestan and Kabardino Balkaria.[1]

ENDNOTE-APPENDIX I

1. Evidence available from the NAC official website, *nac.gov/ru.*

www.ingramcontent.com/pod-product-compliance
Lightning Source LLC
Chambersburg PA
CBHW071115280526
45787CB00003B/1061